AF478304

# SONGS
# FOR
# SIMPLETONS

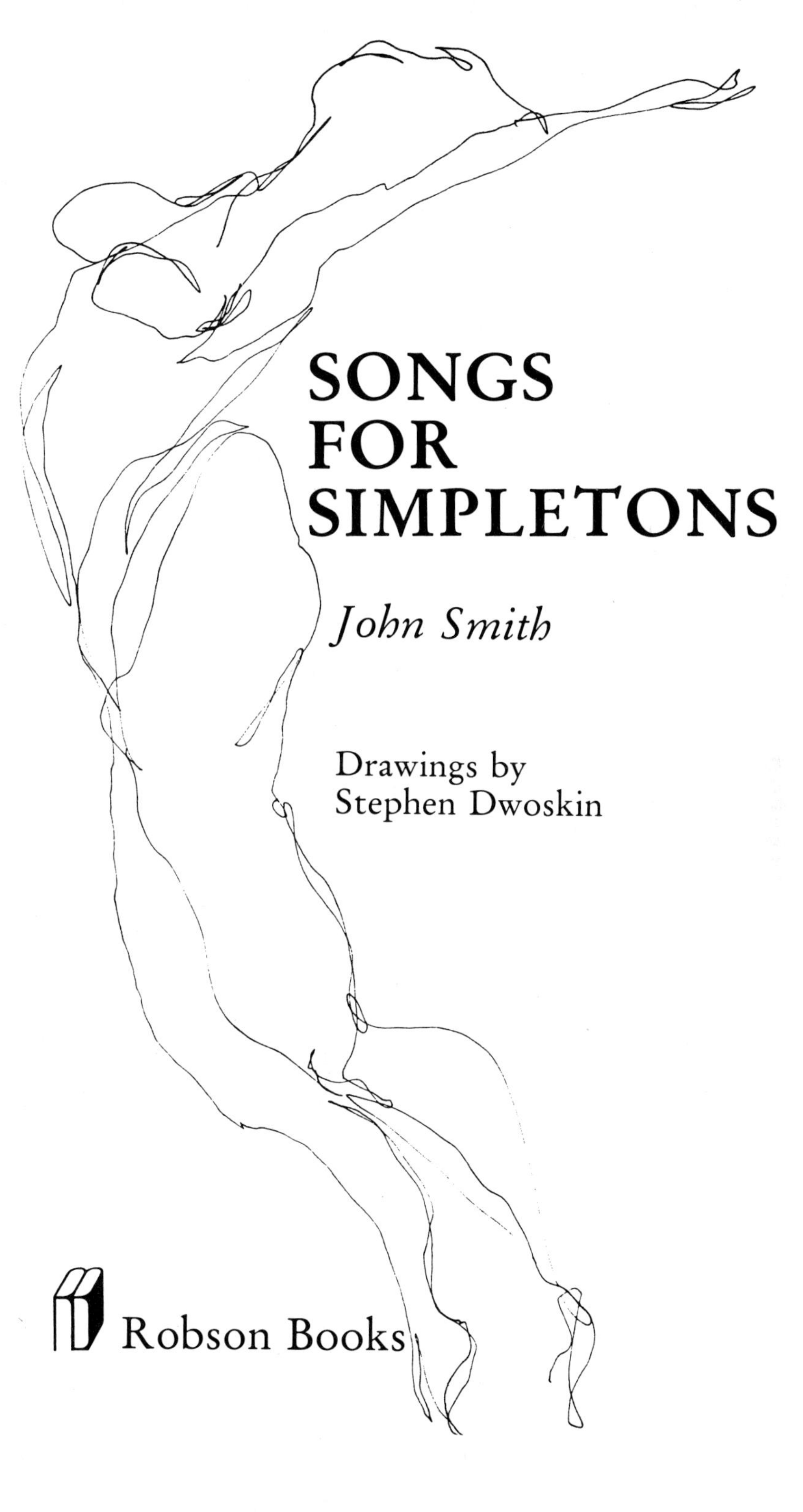

# SONGS FOR SIMPLETONS

*John Smith*

Drawings by
Stephen Dwoskin

Robson Books

FIRST PUBLISHED IN GREAT BRITAIN IN 1984 BY
ROBSON BOOKS LTD., BOLSOVER HOUSE, 5–6
CLIPSTONE STREET, LONDON W1P 7EB. COPY-
RIGHT © 1984 JOHN SMITH.

**British Library Cataloguing in Publication Data**

Smith, John
   Songs for simpletons
   I. Title
   821.914   PR6069.M/
   ISBN 0-86051-268-1



Reproduced, printed and bound in Great Britain by
Hazell Watson & Viney Limited,
Member of the BPCC Group,
Aylesbury, Bucks

# FIRST SET

# ONE

"I plucked an apple from a tree"
  Said Jack "Midsummer's night,
And held it up for all to see,
  'Twas such a pretty sight,
For one side shone as black as black,
  The other white as white."

"It was the moonlight changed it so
  And caused that curious sheen"
Said Jill "For nowhere can there grow
  Such fruit as you have seen"
Then Jack "It changed as through the leaves
  The sun strode in between,

And stabbed the apple with its blade,
  Whereat the strange fruit bled,
And in an instant through the shade
  A terrible ichor spread
Until the apple that I held
  Shone one contiguous red."

Then Jill sank down and, weeping, tried
  Among the green leaves curled
Her small shape in their cave to hide
  While the brute day unfurled
Its gorgeous panoply around
  The apple of the world.

*TWO*

Jill said "Look where the floor of Heaven
   With stars is thick inlaid."
"And yet" said Jack "It seems they all
   Shine in this mossy glade."
Then both upon that turf sank down
   And Love's strange music played.

But as they crooned through that sweet night
   The stars began to fade
As if the very songs they sang
   All Heaven had betrayed,
Till from that dream of Love they woke
   And rose up all dismayed.

"Ah, see!" Howled Jack "Where bitter rain
   Poxes my face like tears,
And thunderous blasts instead of songs
   Deafen my wounded ears."
Said Jill "The cankerous roses pierce
   My breast with thorny spears."

Then as the stars like candle-flames
   Guttered in yon rich sky,
The Angel of the Lord flew down
   Like any peeping spy,
And through God's envy turned that glade
   Into a nauseous sty.

# *THREE*

Said Jill "I saw an Angel fly
  With gold wings from the vault of Heaven,
Its eyes were dazzling as the sky,
  The stars within its hair were seven,
And as it flew such music rang
I thought the host of Heaven sang."

Laughed Jack "Such foolish mysteries
  With which your head is so beguiled
Are no more than those fantasies
  That calm and charm a fretful child.
Better that you should spin and know
Life's harsh realities below."

Then Jill grew silent, but the day
  That gleamed so golden in the morn,
Like an old winding sheet turned grey,
  A dull shroud waiting to be worn.
So Jack leaned down and took her hand
And said "Too soon you'll understand."

And led her where a dead thing lay,
  And flies all golden on the wing
Swarmed down to feed on that decay;
  And said "You'll hear no Angel sing
But only this foul scavenging hum
When flies upon your carcase come."

Then Jill cried loud and hid her face
  To hear what late had sung so fair
Buzz in that stinking charnel place,
  And brushed the stars from out her hair
And freed her hand and fled from Jack
And would not, though he called, turn back.

# *FOUR*

"I plucked an apple from a tree"
  Said Jill "Midwinter's night;
And its bright sheen enchanted me
  Enticing me to bite,
Till on my tongue its juice spilled out
  And filled me with delight.

The sweet flesh in my mouth I rolled,
  Its savour was so rare,
And naked through the orchard strolled
  Until I reached the lair,
Deep in the wood, of that smooth worm
  And boldly entered there."

Whereat Jack heaved his sweating shape
  And stretched his slavering jaw
Then sank his teeth fast in her nape
  And smashed Jill to the floor,
Then munched that bitter apple through,
  Down to its rotten core.

But as engorged, Jack, sated, slept,
  Slyly a black pip fell,
And tendrils like dead fingers crept
  Out of its poisonous shell,
Till round the walls, the roof, the door,
  Bloomed all the flowers of Hell.

A narrow path ran to the West,
  As narrow to the East
And North and South, and at each gate
  Snorted a monstrous beast,
And vultures of the avenging Lord
  Assembled for the feast.

Then bold Jack trembled in his fur
  And, faint, Jill hid her face,
Crying "What prayer may loose us from
  This sacrilegious place,
That was so fair, but now is foul,
  Mauled by our hearts' disgrace."

"It was your whimpering love" cried Jack
  That fetched us to this ill."
"It was the lecherous beast that roared
  Within your heart" cried Jill
"That prowled and prowled within its cage
  Nor ever would lie still."

Then Jack plucked out his eyes like stones,
  And from their sockets shone
A light black as Eternity
  Now his poor sight was gone,
Red as the boiling tears of blood
  That hung, his cheeks upon.

And Jill raised up her hands and tore
  From her soft mouth her tongue,
When from that chasm poured a hymn
  That never on earth was sung;
Such sound as only silence knows
  When Death's last bell is rung.

Then round them, leaf by leaf, the wood
    Withered, the sky drew back
Where, in that fathomless pit of Space
    The sulphurous sun burned black,
And nevermore in God's bad time
    Shall man find Jill or Jack.

# SECOND SET

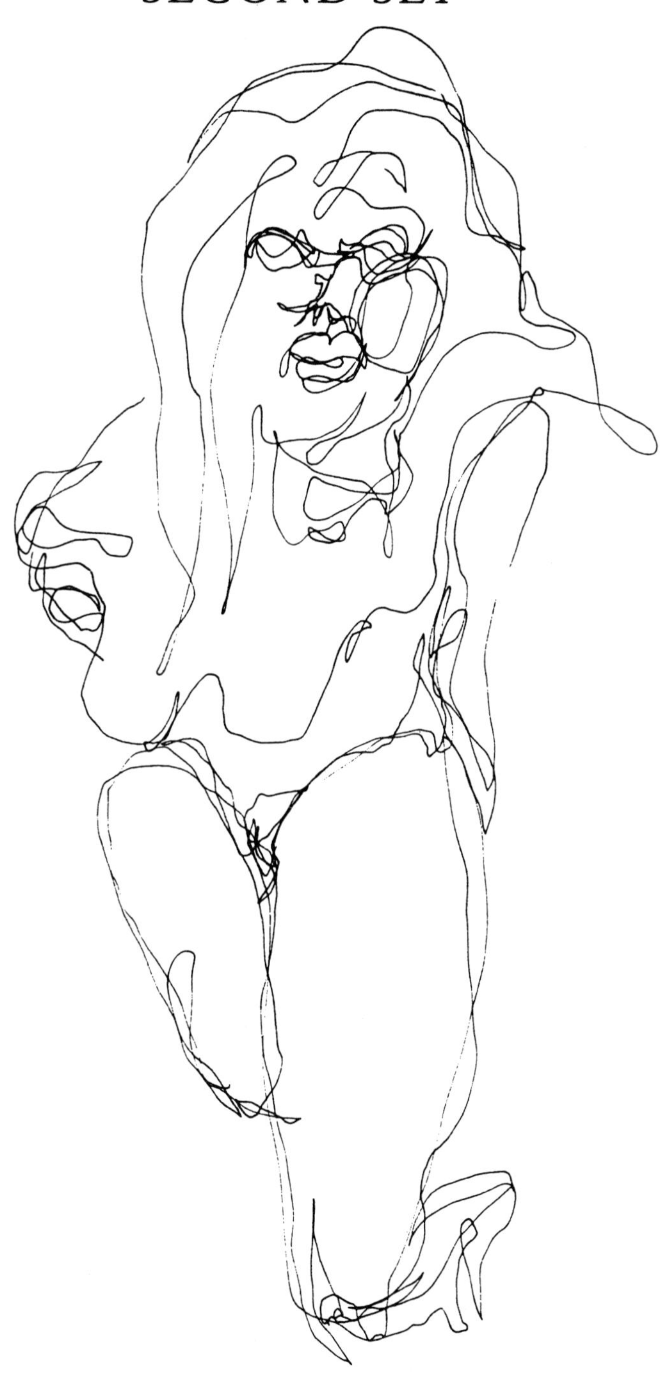

# ONE

Lo! The snorting coursers
Who trample and make known.
Who strike sparks of fire.
Who scour and make known.

You struck me. You said "Hide from my wrath."
I would not hide. I offered you my face. I said
"I will run before you, seeking no shelter."

You struck me. You said "Flee from my anger."
I laughed. I said "Your fury is like thorns,
The brambles tear at my breast, yet I will not hide."

You bore down upon me. I was crushed
By the meteors rushing, the lone stars floating,
By the Angels hastening.

You cried "I will seek you out
By the snorting coursers
Who strike sparks of fire,
Who trample and make known."

*Yet what is the calamity?*

# TWO

You said "Open your hands;
Your fingers sparkle."
I opened my hands.

I said "See, it is the stars."
I offered the stars to you. I said
"Take them; they are yours."

You said "Open your hands;
Your palms glow with light."
I opened my hands.

I said "See, it is the moon."
I offered the moon to you. I said
"Take it; it is yours."

You said "Open your hands;
Your hands burn with fire."
I opened my hands.

I said "See, it is the sun."
I offered the sun to you. I said
"Take it; it is yours."

You said "Open your hands;
Your fists tremble and jerk."
I opened my hands.

I said "It is Life."
I offered Life to you. I said
"Take it; it is yours."

You said "Open your hands;
Your knuckles close upon night."
I opened my hands.

I said "It is night. It is Death."
I offered it to you. I said
"It is night. It is Death.

Take it; it is yours."

# *THREE*

It is pitiful. I loved you.
You said "What is my name?"

I loved you. I said "It is pity."
You smiled. You said "What is my name?"

I loved you. I said "It is what it is;
I cannot speak it." You raised your arms.

I pressed the spike through your wrist.
You said "The sky. The sky." I kissed you.

You cried out "The water is sand!"
I licked the tears from your face.

I have eaten you in my mind
And my head is an enormous stone

Round and enormous.
My head is filled with the dying of the world.

"What is my name?" Over and over.
"What is my name?" "Love me."

# *FOUR*

You said "The taste of earth is sweet,
Kneel upon the earth and touch it."

I said "The taste of water is sweet."

You said "The taste of air is sweet,
Open your mouth and drink the words of the wind."

You said "Press your body to the earth,
Your mouth to its mouth, your tongue to its tongue."

You said "Cast your body upon the wind,
For the air, it is the Quick, the Spirit, the Holy Ghost."

I said "I will lave my limbs with water."

For the taste of water is sweet
The taste of earth is sweet
And the taste of air is sweet.

## *FIVE*

You said "Shall I pluck you a leaf
Shall I cull you a flower
Shall I offer you water
The water of Love
Shall I proffer you wine?"

> You shall pluck me no leaf
> You shall cull me no flower
> For the water you offer
> The water of Love
> Already is mine.

I said "Will you pluck me a leaf
Will you cull me a flower
Will you offer me water
The water of Love
Will you proffer me wine?"

> I will pluck you no leaf
> I will cull you no flower
> For the water you seek
> The water of Love
> Already is yours, not mine.

# THIRD SET

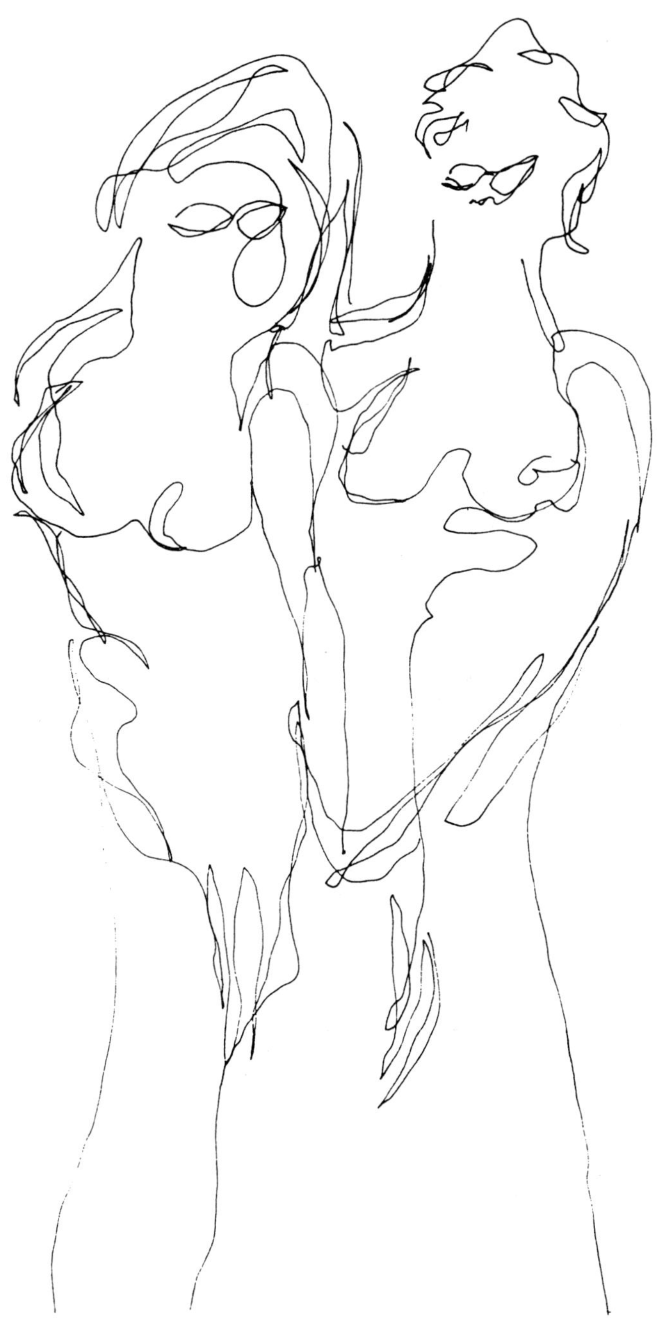

# ONE

"They have cut my little finger"
  "They have stuck me with a thorn,
Piercing my feet to let the blood
  Of one who'll not be born."

"They have burnt my hands with charcoal"
  "They have stabbed my feet with briars"
Cried Jack, cried Jill "And see, how red
  Swirl up the ravening fires."

"My ears are stopped with cinders"
  "My hair with glass is shorn"
Cried Jack, cried Jill "To please the ghost
  Of one who'll not be born."

But then within those snarling flames
  A babe all burning bright
Sprang up to pity Jack and Jill
  And save them from their plight.

Sang he "I'll pluck the poisonous thorn,
  And quench the cinder's pain,
Until such torment unto love
  Never shall come again."

But as he spoke, St. Paul rose up
  And like damnation roared
"Begone bright babe, Love's innocence
  Never shall be restored."

And took from out his glorious robe
  A wicked scourge as thin
As his pursed lips, and round the thongs
  Was twined the small word *'sin'*

"Alas!" shrieked Jack "My flesh that burned,
    Never so sore did smart."
And "Oh! Alas!" cried Jill "such wounds
    Did never rack my heart."

At which from out his withered Heaven
    That babe of Christ's good grace
Fled to the furthest holes of Time
    To hide his pitiful face.

Nor could Jack leap the snorting fire
    Nor brave Jill breast the wave
That raged above, around, below,
    And sealed them in their grave.

# *TWO*

Said Jill to Jack "I hatch a nest
  Of little eagles in my breast."
Said Jack to Jill "How proud the sky
  Will hang above us when they fly."

"And yet" said Jill "I'd sooner Love's
  Rare warmth would bear me turtle doves."
Whereat Jack frowned and struck Jill's face:
  "Such weakness harbours man's disgrace;

Love is a plaything of one hour,
  Man's fate is magnified through power;
Pride drives the weak and strong apart,
  Love's but the dalliance of art."

Jill's heart when those proud birds were flown
  Seemed in her breast a funeral stone,
For as she watched in her dismay
  The eagles turned to birds of prey

From their high eminence above
  Swooping upon the lowly dove.
It seemed their talons, stretched to kill,
  Savaged the trembling flesh of Jill.

But Jack, exultant in the sun,
  Felt his hot blood like lava run,
Nor could he from those bitter years
  Embrace poor Jill or staunch her tears.

Yet when Jack's pride at last was stripped,
  By Death's cold shears his pinnions clipped,
From the black depths of that deep well
  Not one redemptive teardrop fell.

# THREE

Said Jack "I will not play or sing,
  Nor cherish you with curious art."
Said Jill "How will you then convey
  The love you bear me in your heart?"

Said Jack "Such processes confirm
  Not Love, but Art's beguiling lies;
Words but expose the devious man,
  Silence encompasses the wise."

Said Jill "I then shall only give
  Myself, undecked by woman's stuff:
Plain, naked, simple, pure." Said Jack
  "Such singular beauty is enough."

But one day round their serious house
  They saw two flirting chancers run;
It seemed the moon sang from her hair
  And from his garrulous mouth, the sun.

It seemed as though the stars shone out,
  Fire-opals burning at mid-day,
And flowers more rich than Angels' wings
  Alighted on each emerald spray.

Then those grave lovers Jack and Jill
  Spying such trivial playthings there
Turned back, each musing if, at last,
  Love's lies bring joy; Love's truths despair.

# FOUR

Said Jill "The windows in the shops
   Flaunt models in their nakedness;
They have no milk within their breasts
   Nor do they suffer man's distress."

"Their arms" said Jack "Akimbo lie;
   From their bald pates the hair is torn,
And yet they make no grievous moan,
   Who die not, nor were ever born."

But Jill, observing them displayed
   Like dead beasts in a slaughter place
Trembled, and felt the world spin round
   And crushed her hands upon her face

And would have fallen but for Jack
   Who, laughing, held her in his arms
And crooned such comfort as would keep
   Her safe through all the world's alarms.

Yet, even as he cradled her,
   The broken dummies mocked his gaze
Until he felt his blood run hot,
   His love-filled eyes with lust ablaze.

And in that instant flung Jill down
   As if she were a doll to break
And, like those vacant witnesses,
   Out of his nightmare would not wake.

In the black pit in which they fell
   Eros alone observed that rape
Which done, Jack fled, nor cried to see
   Jill's violated limbs agape.

Said Jill "Along these bitter streets
  I see old men in tatters walk;
The filth along the gutter runs
  Less vile than their foul, toothless talk."

"And I" said Jack "In this same town
  Recoil from doorways where grey hags
Lean out to lure me into rooms
  Where they will shuffle from their rags."

Then both fell silent, and the day
  Shuddered as though the sun grew ill
And with its leprous fingers groped
  To blight the love of Jack and Jill.

Yet where those flowers of evil bloomed,
  Pale lilies festering in their moat,
Jack felt the web of Jill's gold hair
  Like Melisande's upon his throat;

While Jill saw, rising from those rags
  Jack like an armoured Titan stride,
And laughed as through the gorgeous town
  He marched to name her as his bride.

She trembled as he sang aloud
  "My friends I claim her as my queen"
The crowd's astonished eyes grew wide:
  Never had they such beauty seen.

And Jill then echoed Jack's bold song
  Crying "He, too, shall be my king."
Then all the multitude that thronged
  The simple square began to sing,

And led the lovers hand in hand:
    To chalets built of wood and glass?
To brothels thick with graveyard mould?
    Who knows which fate may come to pass?

All fictions end, as end they must;
    Nor Jack Nor Jill till life was through
Could from their trance of loving know
    Which tale was false; which tale was true.

# FOURTH SET

# ONE

I said "Will you sing out for me?"
And your voice said 'Yes' and sang
In delight of Speaking.

You said "Will you sing out for me?"
And my eyes said 'Yes' and sang
In delight of Seeing.

I said "Will you sing out for me?"
And your ears said 'Yes' and sang
In delight of Hearing.

You said "Will you sing out for me?"
And my mind said 'Yes' and sang
In delight of Knowing.

In delight of Speaking
And in delight of Seeing
I will sing out to you.

In delight of Hearing
And in delight of Knowing
I will sing out to you.

# *TWO*

"If to this Heaven" You said,
  "It cometh by the North,
I will sit at the South
  So I may embrace thee."

"If to this Heaven" I said,
  "It cometh by the South,
I will sit at the North
  So I may embrace thee."

"If to this Heaven" You said,
  "It cometh by the West,
I will sit at the East
  So I may embrace thee."

"If to this Heaven" I said,
  "It cometh by the East,
I will sit at the West
  So I may embrace thee."

You said "I am strong in my mouth,
  And my nostrils quiver;
My nostrils quiver
  When you come to me upon the winds."

I said "I snuff the wind of the East
  By his head, and grasp
The breezes of the South,
  My hands upon its hair."

You said "I will descend from Heaven,
  Robed in the flame of my mouth."
I said "I will embrace thee in peace, and drive
  The fiends from the mouth of thy paths."

But who then is this? Who then is this
  Who strides in, saying:

*Let the state of the shining ones*
  *Be given unto you,*
*And the quietness of heart*
  *Instead of cakes and ale.*

## *THREE*

See, I bring you water in a cup.
Drink the water I offer you.
And little cakes; eat of the little cakes.

Why do you turn from me? The well
Dries; the cakes blacken. You eat
Nothing; neither do you drink.

> Though I thirst I cannot drink.
> Though I hunger I cannot eat;
> Neither of the water, nor the little cakes.

> Though my belly swells with want
> And my arms and legs grow thin
> And my eyes focus upon nothing.

I will spill the water on the ground
For the sand to drink; while the cakes
Turn to stones in the desert.

The great wind blows over the desert
In its barrenness; my mouth chokes
In a furnace of sand.

> See, I bring you water in a cup.
> Drink the water I offer you.
> And little cakes; eat of the little cakes.

> Why do you turn from me? The well
> Dries; the cakes blacken. You eat
> Nothing; neither do you drink.

## *FOUR*

You said, walking among the flowers,
  "Your beauty never from nature came,
Nor did Pygmalion shape your limbs
  Nor Loge set your hair aflame;

A Pearl so spotless, bright and pure,
  Could none contrive, of human fame,
Nor regulations, laws, or art,
  Bear such a Pearl, so free from shame."

I said "You speak as though a dream
  Had entered in to drug you where
The flowers, as night comes on, exhale
  Their scent like Opium in the air.

It is your visionary love
  Alone that, lighting on my hair,
Catches the threads and, in your eyes,
  Makes those dark strands like candles flare."

"Then let us live within this dream
  If dream it is, and never stray"
You said; but I "Never so sweet
  Night's dream but shudders into day,

In which on actual winds we drift
  And tides that sweep us where they flow;
Such Heavenly bliss as you espouse,
  Breathes not round mortals here below."

You said "Your truths cannot gainsay
  My love, O Pearl of rich renown,
Not dreamt, but real as these flowers are,
  Which only from our love is grown."

So I, who would not wake your dream
  Grew silent, but beyond your face,
Heard Time's relentless engines grind
  Through the vast mindlessness of Space.

*FIVE*

You said "If you turned to me, somewhere in the world,
With arms outstretched, your fingertips groping,
The dark space between would narrow, bringing me close."
"If you could know! If you could only know!" I said.

And I said "When I weep for you, somewhere in the world,
Your hand carresses my face, and your lips
Move on my eyelids to dispel that anguish."
"If I could know! If I could only know!" You said

When the thick rust invades us, silting our blood,
And we blow out the flickering world like a candle flame
The poisonous smoke will clear on the side of waking.
"If we could know! If we could only know!" We said.

# FIFTH SET

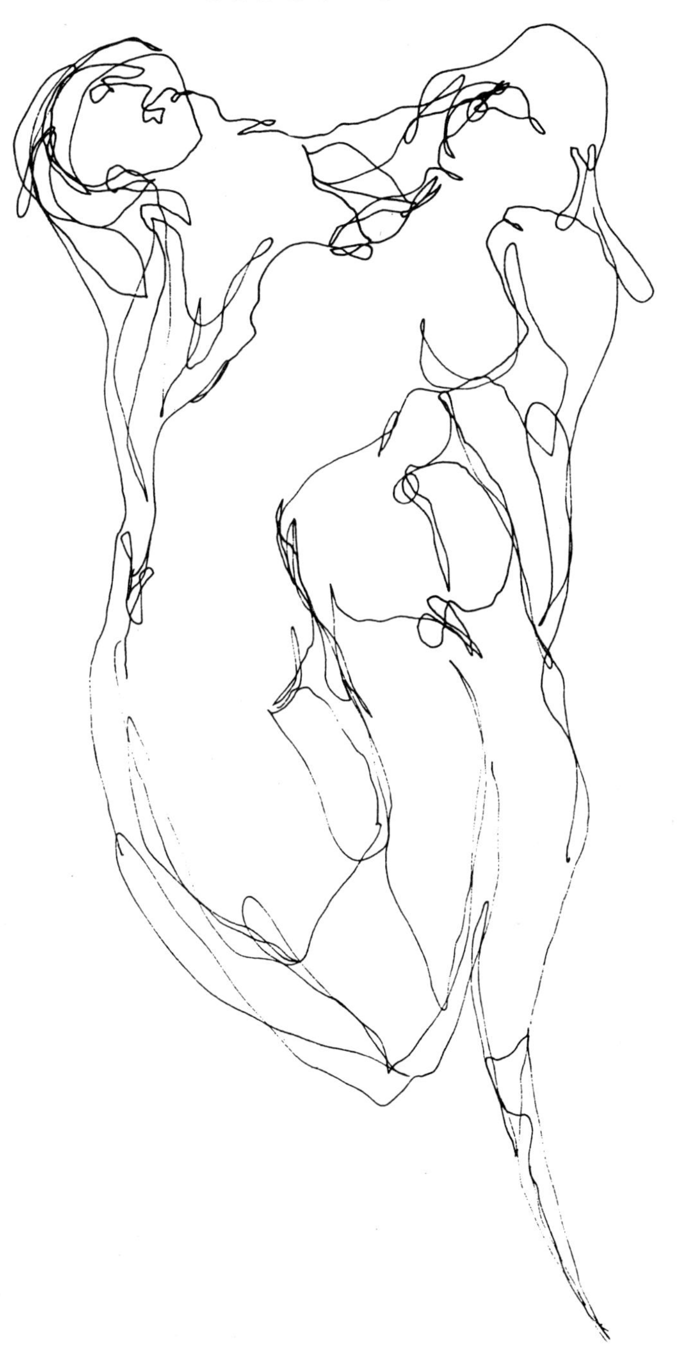

# ONE

"I saw the river burn" said Jack.
 Said Jill "I saw the sea on fire
Like a tall raging chimney stack,
 And as I watched the flames leapt higher

Than Heaven's gate." Said Jack "I saw
 The mountain like a fountain run
And the black rocks as water pour."
 Said Jill "I saw the scorching sun

Freeze in the sky to ice." Jack said
 "I felt the stars like mirrors spill
Sharp crystal splinters in my head."
 "You lie! You never did!" said Jill.

And took his head and clawed and clawed
 Digging until her nails ran red
Where in his skull her fingers bored.
 "You never, never did!" Jill said.

*TWO*

"Put on these dancing shoes." Said Jack.
  "Why should I skip for you?" Laughed Jill.
On either side the ferny track
  The grass ran crimson down the hill.

Said Jack "How strange that this same knife
  Which sprang red poppies from the earth
Will not now coax my Jill to life
  And sharpen her dull flesh to birth.

I'll pluck the poppies dripping red
  And taste their petals on my tongue
And drink the elixir" Jack said
  "Of Jill who would not dance when young.

Until her blood as rich as wine
  That would not jig or jog alone
Consorts and gambols, teaching mine
  A dance no man before has know."

# *THREE*

"My love" said Jack "Is of a birth
  As rare . . ." Said Jill . . . "And strange and High."
"It fills" said Jack "The earth and air."
  "It fills" said Jill "The sea and sky."

"Eyes cannot see two perfect loves."
  Said Jill "For there's a wicked cage
Where vicious jealousy disproves
  Eternal bliss, and passions rage."

Said Jack "But I for good or ill
  Would make our world one planisphere;
Ourselves conjoined, complete." Cried Jill
  "Such compress can but crush, my dear."

And turning, took a jagged stone
  And struck Jack dead and left him there;
Then, laughing, danced away alone
  Through sea and sky and earth and air.

*FOUR*

"Dear, let me watch you brush your hair."
  Said Jack "As fine as gossamer."
Laughed Jill "What poet's language rare
  Is that? My hair is rough as fur

On any mangy beast." "Ah, no"
  Said Jack "You cannot see or feel
As I, nor understand, nor know."
  "But if I took a knife of steel"

Said Jill "And cut it from the roots,
  And placed it lifeless in your hand
'Twould look no different from a brute's."
  Cried Jack "You will not understand."

Then, leaping, wrenched those tresses out
  From Jill's bright head, and tore and tore,
Until his little seeds of doubt
  Upon that skull could find no more;

But, standing in that swathe of hair
  That stank like rank grass where he stood,
Jack smelt the thick and pungent air
  Of dead beasts in their bloody wood.

*FIVE*

"I peered into a grave last night."
  Said Jack "and saw you lying there."
"And were my bones" said Jill "as white
  As snowflakes drifting down the air?"

"Your bones" said Jack "were cracked and green."
  "And were my eyes" said Jill "still blue?"
"Your eyes were nowhere to be seen"
  Said Jack "but pits where earth showed through."

"And did you love me then" asked Jill
  "As now you say you love me here?
And, more, will worship me until
  The lilting seas gang dry and sere?"

"Alas!" Cried Jack "I saw your flesh
  Corrupted lie, that was so rich,
Your hair that does my heart enmesh,
  Uncouth as ragwort in a ditch;

And when I saw you in that pit
  I leapt within its gaping maw
And clasped your shape and ransacked it."
  Said Jill "But I had fled before

You ever found that stinking hole."
  And leaning, placed her lips upon
His mouth, her lips as hot as coal.
  "Nor will you find where I have gone."

Against such fire his lips turned black,
  Blacker than Angels scorched by sin;
"But when I come at last" screamed Jack
  "Open the door and let me in.

49

Open the door, by day or night!"
  Mocked Jill "You'll never find that house,
For you must love in Love's despite
  That will not your desire espouse."

Then Jack leapt up the naked hill
  And scratched the stars from out God's face
But could not, though he roamed, find Jill,
  Through times and Time; through space and Space.

# *A NOTE ON THE REFERENCES*

*Songs for Simpletons* is not intended to be read as an allegory of love but it does concern itself (as may be detected by the ambiguous pun in the last line of Section 3, song 4) with the dichotomy between Eros and Agape. Although most of the allusions, quotations or adaptations will be readily appreciated, there are certain references which are rather more obscure; for the sake of completeness I list them all below.

1st Set:   2   "Look where the floor of heaven
Is thick inlaid with patines of bright gold."
*Shakespeare: The Merchant of Venice*

"O Love they die/In yon rich sky
*Alfred, Lord Tennyson: The Princess*

The Angel of the Lord came down/And glory shone around.
*Christmas Carol: While Shepherds Watched*

   3   "She had three lilies in her hand
And the stars in her hair were seven"
*Dante Gabriel Rossetti: The Blessed Damozel*

   3   "When golden flies upon my carcass come."
*Richard Eberhart: title of poem*

2nd Set:   1   The Snorting Coursers, etc., is adapted from Sûrah C
What is the Calamity from Sûrah CI
By the Meteors Rushing, etc., from Sûrah LXXIX
*Marmaduke Pickthall: The Meaning of the Glorious Koran*

   2   Although the scenario is the Crucifixion "What

is my name?" is a repeated question in the
Egyptian *Book of the Dead*.

4    The taste of Earth is Sweet, etc., is adapted from
the *I Ching*.


3rd Set    1    Rituals of the cutting off of the little finger, and
the placing of hot charcoal in his palm, of a man
who dies childless, is reported by Sir James
Frazer; similarly the rituals of the cutting off of a
woman's hair with broken glass and the piercing
of her feet with thorns if she has died shortly
after giving birth (here a stillbirth) is related by
the same authority. Great efforts were made to
prevent the return of the dead in the form of
revengeful ghosts by the setting up of barriers of
fire and water which they could not cross.
*Sir James Frazer: The fear of the dead in primitive
religions.*

1    "A pretty babe all burning bright/Did in the air
appear"
*Robert Southwell: The Burning Babe*

2    "Who feels his warm heart hatched into a nest
Of little eagles and young doves, whose high
Flights scorn the lazy dust and things that die."
*Richard Crashaw: An Apologie for the foregoing
Hymne*

4    "What were all the world's alarms"
*W. B. Yeats: A Lullaby.*

5    "Fourmillante cité, cité pleine de rêves,
Où le spectre en plein jour raccroche le passant!
Les mystères partout coulent comme des sèves
Dans les canaux étroits du colosse puissant." etc.,
*Charles Baudelaire: Les Sept Vieillards – Les
Fleurs du Mal*

"Ces monstres disloqués furent jadis des
femmes, Éponine ou Laïs!"
*Charles Baudelaire: Les Petites Vieilles – Les
Fleurs du Mal*

Un beau matin, chez un peuple fort doux, un
homme et une femme superbes criaient, sur
la place publique:
"Mes amis, mes amis, je veux qu'elle soit reine, je
veux qu'elle soit reine!"
"Je veux être reine, être reine, être reine!"
Elle riait et tremblait."
*Arthur Rimbaud; Royauté – Les Illuminations*

"Des chalets de crystal et de bois"
*Arthur Rimbaud: Villes – Les Illuminations*

4th Set:  1   The source is the *Brihadaranyaka Upanishad*

        2   The source is the *Egyptian Book of the Dead:
trans. A. Wallis Budge.*

        3   As above

        4   "O maskeleȝ Perle, *in* perleȝ pure,
þat bereȝ," qu*o*þ I, "pe þerle of prys,
Quo formed þe þy fayre fygure?
þat wroȝt þy wede, he watȝ ful wys;
þy beaute com neu*er* of nature;
Pymalyon paynted neu*er* þy vys;
                . . . *Anon: Pearl LXIII*

"O perle," quoþ I, "of rych renou*n*,
So watȝ hit me dere þat þou con deme
I*n* þys v*er*ay avysyou*n*!
                . . . *Anon: Pearl XCIX*

        5   The source is "Ego te per omne quod datum
mortalibus . . ."
*Paulinus of Nola: Ad Ausonium*

5th Set:  3  "My Love is of a birth as rare/As tis for object
              strange and high."
              *Andrew Marvell: The Definition of Love*

              "Unless the giddy Heaven fall
              And earth some new convulsion tear;
              And, us to joyn, the world should all
              Be cramp't into a *planisphere*."
              *Andrew Marvell: The Definition of Love*

          4  "And sang within the bloody wood/When
              Agamemnon cried aloud."
              *T. S. Eliot: Sweeney Among the Nightingales.*

          5  "And I will luve thee still, my dear/Till a' the
              seas gang dry."
              *Robert Burns: My Luve is like a Red, Red rose.*